AN UNDERWATER OCEAN ADVENTURE

BABY & TODDLER COLOR BOOKS

Speedy Publishing LLC
40 E. Main St. #1156
Newark, DE 19711
www.speedypublishing.com

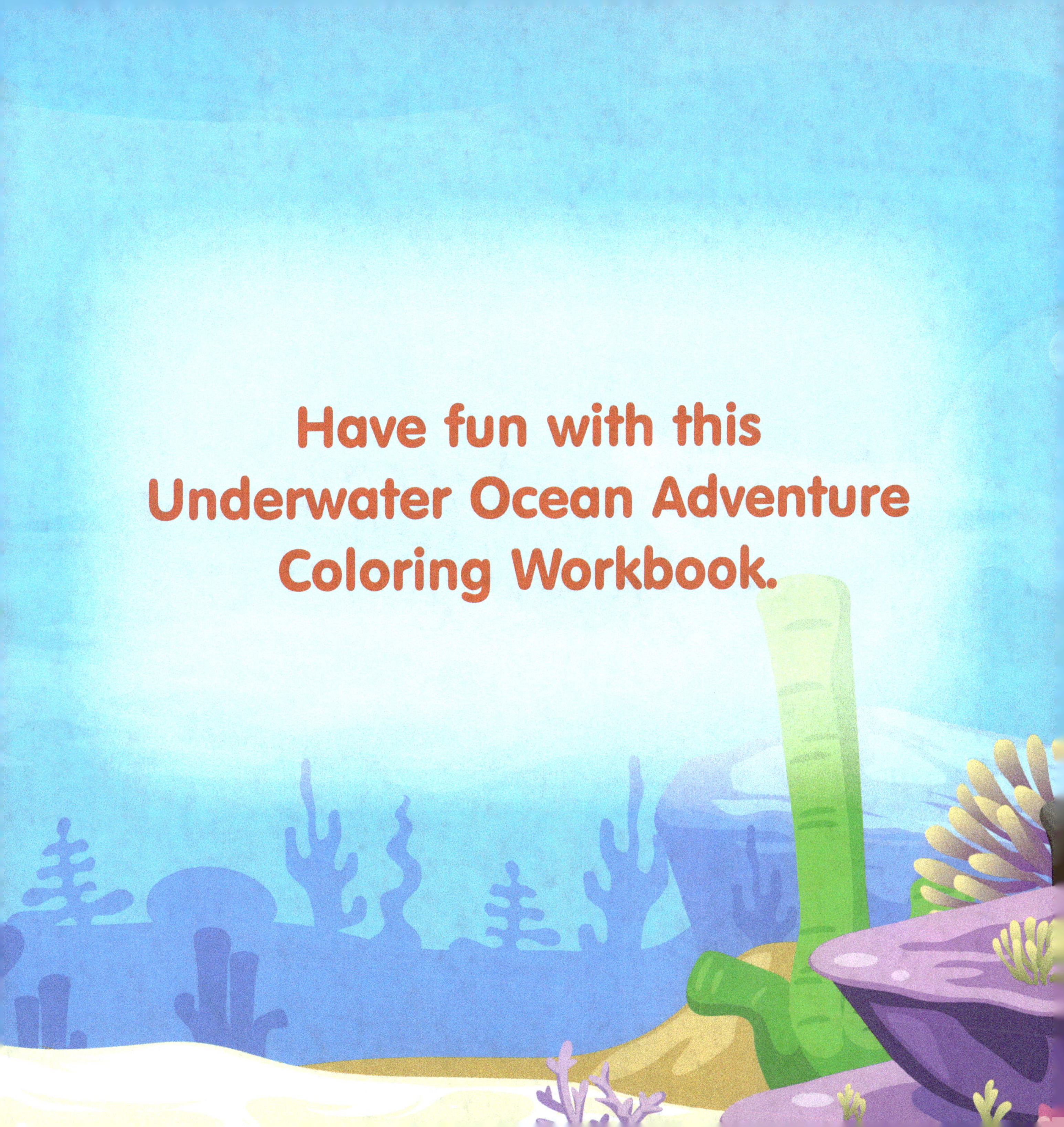

Have fun with this
Underwater Ocean Adventure
Coloring Workbook.

Coloring Exercises with color swatches

Coloring Exercises without color swatches

10
11

Connect the Dots and Color

Color the Picture

Did you enjoy coloring?
Keep it up!

www.ingramcontent.com/pod-product-compliance
Lightning Source LLC
LaVergne TN
LVHW060509170826
845677LV00026B/1704
9798869443694